Letters to a
New School Teacher

Letters to a
New School Teacher

advice from
America's best educators

edited by
Jeanne Devlin

THE ROADRUNNER PRESS
OKLAHOMA CITY

THE ROADRUNNER PRESS
P.O. Box 2564
Oklahoma City, OK 73101
www.TheRoadRunnerPress.com

ISBN: 978-1-937054-10-6

Library of Congress Control Number: 2011914201

10 9 8 7 6 5 4 3 2

*For my mother, who never met
a child without potential*

*For Michelle Shearer,
the 2011 National Teacher of the Year*

*And for all the many teachers everywhere,
who refused to give up on a child ...
when everyone else had*

Introduction

This little book carries a big message: great American teachers exist — and they can be found working in grade schools, middle schools, and high schools in rural towns and big cities in all fifty states. What they know about teaching could very well help a young or new or aspiring teacher you know. If so, we hope you will share this book with them.

As for our contributors, they come from one of the most competitive awards programs in the world: The United States' National Teacher of the Year Program. Every single one of this year's fifty state teachers of the year took the time to respond, though you will find advice from only forty-nine inside. That's because great teachers play by the rules, and the rules of the program make it difficult for the National Teacher of the Year, once chosen, to participate in outside projects.

That said, we could not leave out the 2011 National Teacher of the Year, Michelle Shearer of Urbana High School in Ijamsville, Maryland, so we dedicate this book in part to her, as a thank you for her service to the children of Maryland.

— Jeanne Devlin

Table of Contents

Be Kind

Annice M. Brave

. . . .

Illinois Teacher of the Year

. . . .

11th & 12th English, Journalism

. . . .

Alton High School

. . . .

Alton, Illinois

Your students may not remember any of the words you say or the facts you teach them, but they will never forget how you made them feel. The kind words you say, the nonverbal messages you send, and the advice you give to each child will never appear on a standardized test, but your students will always remember those moments, for they are the important lessons, and students will carry them into the future.

— Annice M. Brave

*"Warmth is the vital element
for the growing plant and
the soul of the child."*

— Carl Jung,
Swiss psychiatrist

Be Original

Curtis Chandler

. . . .

Kansas Teacher of the Year

. . . .

8th Language Arts

. . . .

Wamego Middle School

. . . .

Wamego, Kansas

Do not waste your time figuring out how to teach students to do something that has already been done. Instead, invest every resource and ounce of your energy as a teacher into inspiring your students to be creative and to design something new, useful, and inventive.

After researching unique restaurants across the country — including one that lifts guest several hundred feet in the air before serving them gourmet dishes in a glass room with a view over the city — my students were asked to create a novel restaurant that couldn't be found anywhere else in the world.

They used their creativity and writing skills to compose descriptive, narrative, expository, and technical pieces about every aspect of their chosen restaurant.   They worked harder than I can ever remember seeing students work.   When asked why the usual challenges and difficulties of the writing process seemed to disappear with this assignment, they answered: "We were having so much fun that we didn't even realize how much work we were doing."

Mission accomplished.

— Curtis Chandler

Be Prepared

Amanda McAdams

. . . .

Arizona Teacher of the Year

. . . .

10th English / 9th - 12th Student Government

. . . .

Apollo High School

. . . .

Glendale, Arizona

Balance your passion for your students and the content with organization. Show your students how much you care by providing them with meaningful lessons, while also having clear expectations and procedures in place in your classroom. Model what you expect and always have a rubric! (For my students, I make a model for every project, but I also make models for how to answer a question completely, how to pass in absent work, and how to organize an essay — among others.)

— Amanda McAdams

Stefani Cook

. . . .

Idaho Teacher of the Year

. . . .

10th - 12th Business, Technology Education

. . . .

Rigby High School

. . . .

Rigby, Idaho

Never enter your classroom unprepared for the day. Overplan — and make each moment a teachable moment. Remain consistent in all aspects of your teaching, so your students will always know what is expected of them. Expect great things of them, because no matter how high the expectations, given the correct tools and motivation your students will meet and, in many cases, exceed those expectations. They will also come to respect you, their fellow classmates, the subject matter, their environment, and themselves.

— Stefani Cook

*"Education with inert ideas
is not only useless, it is
above all things harmful."*

— Alfred North Whitehead,
English philosopher

Be Relevant

Tyronna Hooker

. . . .

North Carolina Teacher of the Year

. . . .

8th Special Education, Language Arts, Social Studies

. . . .

Graham Middle School

. . . .

Graham, North Carolina

A variable is a value that may change within the scope of a given problem. For your students, you must be the variable that matters. Each child comes to school with different strengths, interests, and needs. Each child has a unique story to be studied and understood. You will not be able to control their family dynamics or background but you can create change in the hours they are with you. The focus of your classroom must be to create life-long learners who will grow up to become socially responsible citizens. Do not allow things outside your circle of influence to prohibit you from being the variable that matters.

— Tyronna Hooker

*"Schoolmasters and parents
exist to be grown out of."*

— John Wolfenden,
British educator

Be a Talent Guide

Matinga Ragatz

. . . .

Michigan Teacher of the Year

. . . .

Global Studies

. . . .

Grand Ledge High School

. . . .

Grand Ledge, Michigan

Think of yourself as a "Talent Guide." Doing so will force you to reevaluate the relevance of every activity in your classroom and to trim away redundant practices — obstacles in your quest to prepare students to take their place in today's economy. Embrace technology to repackage and deliver required content in ways that compel you to act as a facilitator on the sidelines.

Prepare online interactive activities (short demo videos, recorded webinars) that help you deliver the course content in short digestible ways that students can consume on demand and at their own pace. Then, use instructional time to guide relevant discussions, ask tough questions during student presentations, help connect the dots about the content they learn online, watch compelling films, invite speakers and experts from around the world via teleconferences, throw all manner of monkey wrenches into group work to provoke critical thinking and to provide one-on-one differentiated learning.

But be forewarned! This approach to learning is labor intensive, as you will have much to research and prepare. So seek out colleagues who are willing to collaborate and share the workload when preparing creative expert online course content. Many, many failures will mark your quest to guide student talent, but remember that failure is the main ingredient needed to innovate and to continue to push the learning boundaries.

— Matinga Ragatz

Be Yourself

Colleen Works

. . . .

Oregon Teacher of the Year

. . . .

11th - 12th Social Science

. . . .

Corvallis High School

. . . .

Corvallis, Oregon

Love the work — revel in the problems and exult at the solutions. Celebrate the small victories, and throw galas for the large ones. Laugh every day, especially at yourself. Understand that teaching can magnify your foibles; be sure not to take yourself too seriously.

Know that you are embarking on a fabulous journey, and enjoy every moment, especially those that are the most challenging. When you hurt, feel blessed to care so much about your work that you can ache for it.

At the end of the school year, reflect on how far you've traveled and take note not only of how much your students learned, but also of how you have changed and grown — and how much more you understand life because you do this job.

Celebrate that you get paid to be a learner and marvel at what a better person you are now because of the life's work you chose.

— Colleen Works

*"I am not a teacher,
I am an awakener."*

**— Robert Frost,
American poet and teacher**

Maureen Look-Ainsworth

. . . .

Wisconsin Teacher of the Year

. . . .

5th Science / Engineering

. . . .

Horning Middle School

. . . .

Waukesha, Wisconsin

Be yourself. If you love to hike, live it. If you love to read, show it. Whatever your passion is, live it in front of your students. Live by the same high standard that you hold for them. They know you, know about you, and can tell whether you care about them from the very first class.

Remember that you stand as one with the dedicated, compassionate, caring individuals and families that give of their time and energy to make education better for the next generation. Live your life robustly — giving your time, your talent, your energy, and resources.

You will never regret it.

— Maureen Look-Ainsworth

*"Teachers open the door,
but you must enter by yourself."*

— Chinese Proverb

Create a Safe Place

Susan Turnipseed

· ·

South Dakota Teacher of the Year

· ·

4th Technology

· ·

Camelot Intermediate School

· ·

Brookings, South Dakota

Take the time to build community and trust in the classroom. Work with students to establish a secure atmosphere in which all feel safe to offer ideas, take risks, and help others. This sense of community starts the first day of school and develops throughout the year as the level of trust among students grows. The world outside the classroom may often be one of chaos, unkindness, and uncertainty, but when students walk through the door of your classroom let them feel comfortable, accepted, and welcome in a place where routines, boundaries, and procedures provide the security they crave, so all can learn and grow.

— Susan Turnipseed

"The reason teaching has to go on is that children are not born human; they are made so."

— Jacques Barzun,
American cultural historian

Enjoy the Process

Cheryl Conley

. . . .

Florida Teacher of the Year

. . . .

4th Grade / Middle School Science

. . . .

Osceola Magnet Elementary School

. . . .

Vero Beach, Florida

Always remember that learning is a process, not a product. Learning takes time, energy, and effort. Every child has value — build a meaningful relationship with each one. Ask about their hopes and dreams, and encourage them to find their passions and hidden talents.

Get to know their families. On the very first day of school, have them complete a form with their home and parent information as well as information about them, including their birthday. Every time you make a negative phone call home, make a positive call as well.

In the classroom, create an active, engaging environment that encourages risk taking.

Encourage your students to take a leap of faith, to venture into the unknown, and to never surrender in their quest for knowledge. Take risks as a teacher as well: think outside the box and encourage your students to do the same.

Design open-ended lessons that build upon one another. Dress in crazy costumes, laugh, sing, dance, and rap with your students.

When things get tough, please remember: You can do this. Breathe. Look into the faces of your students and remember exactly why you became a teacher.

— Cheryl Conley

"Life is amazing, and the teacher had better prepare himself to be a medium for that amazement."

— Edward Blishen,
British author and teacher

Molly Boyle

. . . .

Iowa Teacher of the Year

. . . .

3rd Grade

. . . .

Brookview Elementary

. . . .

West Des Moines, Iowa

Never lose sight of the fact that you were a learner first . . . and a teacher second. Effective teachers understand that both teaching and learning are complex, dynamic processes that require continuous professional growth.

Read educational literature, pursue advanced degrees, collaborate with colleagues, and, most importantly, learn from your students. They have much to teach you.

— Molly Boyle

Pam Williams

. . . .

Georgia Teacher of the Year

. . . .

Social Sciences

. . . .

Appling County High School

. . . .

Baxley, Georgia

The first year of teaching is a beautifully winding road that combines smooth sailing, blind curves, thrilling peaks, and the occasional speed bump. When navigating the journey: Be flexible. The best planned lesson can fall apart, and life-changing "teachable moments" appear from thin air.

Embrace such gifts of opportunity.

Most importantly, love what you are doing each and every day. You have chosen to teach; you have chosen to make a difference in the lives of young people. Choose to love what you are doing every day, come rain or come shine. Your attitude will largely determine the attitude of each student in your class. Choose to make it a positive day — and let the fun and learning begin!

— Pam Williams

*"A teacher affects eternity;
he can never tell where
his influence stops."*

— Henry Adams,
American writer

Expect Greatness

Stacy McCormack

· ·

Indiana Teacher of the Year

· ·

11th - 12th Physics / Chemistry / Physical Sciences

· ·

Penn High School

· ·

Mishawaka, Indiana

Inspire young people to dream beyond their backgrounds — to reach beyond what they think they can accomplish and to learn to have faith in their own abilities. When you succeed in any one of these things, pause for a moment, take a deep breath, and realize that you have just changed the trajectory of a young person's life . . . and thus the world.

— Stacy McCormack

Adam Gray

. . . .

Massachusetts Teacher of the Year

. . . .

9th, 10th, & 12th Mathematics

. . . .

Monument High School

. . . .

Boston, Massachusetts

Effective teaching starts with the belief that all students — regardless of the obstacles they may face at home or elsewhere — can, should, and will reach the high expectations you set for them. Communicate your commitment to helping your students achieve these expectations by routinely engaging them in solutions-oriented conversations focused on academic achievement and personal growth. Demonstrate your commitment to helping your students by meticulously planning lessons and monitoring their progress.

— Adam Gray

Robert Becker

· ·

Missouri Teacher of the Year

· ·

10th, 11th, & 12th Chemistry, AP Chemistry

· ·

Kirkwood High School

· ·

Kirkwood, Missouri

Starting day one, set the bar high.

Expect failure. Embrace failure. Failure has gotten a bad name, and that's a shame, for it is a far more effective teacher than success. Provide your students plenty of opportunities to fail — and then be patient and supportive as they strive to bounce back! Post this quotation prominently in your classroom:

"Success is a lousy teacher. It seduces smart people into thinking they can't lose."

Then ask your students to guess who said it.

The answer? Bill Gates.

— Robert Becker

*"It takes a whole village
to raise a child."*

— West African Proverb

Include the Village

Lorrie Heagy

. . . .

Alaska Teacher of the Year

. . . .

K - 5th Music / Library

. . . .

Glacier Valley Elementary School

. . . .

Juneau, Alaska

No one teacher has all of the answers. Reach out to your colleagues and community members for inspiration, guidance, and expertise.

Collaborative teaching will not only enliven and diversify instruction, but also remind you that you are never alone.

— Lorrie Heagy

Angie C. Miller

. . . .

New Hampshire Teacher of the Year

. . . .

6th - 8th English / Language Arts

. . . .

Holderness Central School

. . . .

Holderness, New Hampshire

Always remember that your classroom extends beyond its four walls. Parents and the community want to be part of your students' learning. When they are, you will see great success. Bring your teaching out into the community and the greater world into your daily instruction.

Parents will respect and trust you; the local businesses will support you; and your students will learn to serve their community and understand their roots. And in the end, they will thank you for showing them what it means to be part of something bigger than one's self.

— Angie C. Miller

Jeffrey Chou

. . . .

Pennsylvania Teacher of the Year

. . . .

6th Grade

. . . .

Highland Elementary School

. . . .

Abington, Pennsylvania

Become a member of your school community. They say, "It takes a village to raise a child." If you become part of the village, you can help shape it, and that will become one of your most useful tools as a teacher.

— Jeffrey Chou

"Every truth has four corners: as a teacher I give you one corner, and it is for you to find the other three."

— Confucius,
Chinese educator

Know the Child

Julia Williams

. . . .

Louisiana Teacher of the Year

. . . .

9th - 11th Algebra II Gifted

. . . .

Lafayette High School

. . . .

Lafayette, Louisiana

Never underestimate the importance of relationships. Getting to know your students and their parents or guardians creates a positive learning environment where students feel safe and truly cared about.

— Julia Williams

Shelly Moody

. . . .

Maine Teacher of the Year

. . . .

3rd - 5th Grades

. . . .

Williams Elementary School

. . . .

Oakland, Maine

Every child comes to school with a life story. Take the time to know each student as a person and a learner. When you treasure every child's true passions, you can make learning relevant to the child and foster a lifetime of learning.

— Shelly Moody

Birdette Hughey

. . . .

Mississippi Teacher of the Year

. . . .

9th - 11th Algebra I

. . . .

Greenwood High School

. . . .

Greenwood, Mississippi

When you enter your first classroom, you will encounter the most beautiful collage you could ever imagine. This collage will be painted with many talents, strengths, and personalities, as well as the differences that each of your students possess.

Starting your first day, use the tools — learning style assessments, interest inventories, goal-driven conversations — in your toolbox to identify the unique attributes of each of your students. Include what you learn about each student in your lessons and watch how doing so empowers them.

— Birdette Hughey

Cheryl Macy

. . . .

Nevada Teacher of the Year

. . . .

9th - 12th English

. . . .

Carson High School

. . . .

Carson City, Nevada

Always remember teaching is all about human connection. Once my students were assigned to write a letter to their parents. Quiet Armando, who rarely smiled and never did his work, confided to me that he could not do the assignment, because his mother had just died of cancer and his father was in prison.

That knowledge changed everything. This was why school had not been a priority for him, and knowing that made me better able to tailor the assignments to engage him in the days and weeks that followed. Our relationship changed for the better, and he started doing his work.

When a positive rapport exists between teacher and student, students work harder and take more pride in their work — even in the worst of times.

Simple efforts to connect with students on a personal level can make your job much easier . . . and your teaching much more effective.

— Cheryl Macy

"For the mind does not require filling like a bottle, but rather, like wood, only kindling to create in it an impulse to think independently ..."

— Plutarch,
Greek philosopher and author

Elizabeth Smith

. . . .

Oklahoma Teacher of the Year

. . . .

7th Reading

. . . .

Byng Junior High School

. . . .

Ada, Oklahoma

Take the time to get to know each and every one of your students. Remember, it is just as important to know your students as it is to know your subject. Find joy in what you do, and understand that every day you have an opportunity to make a difference.

— Elizabeth Smith

Daniel Leija

. . . .

Texas Teacher of the Year

. . . .

5th Math / Science

. . . .

Gregorio Esparza Accelerated Elementary School

. . . .

San Antonio, Texas

Remember that students do not all learn the same way. Vary your approach. Don't be afraid to get your students up and moving. Stop frequently to check for understanding. Let them take ownership of their learning. Your goal is not to find out if your students are smart. Your goal is to find out how they are smart.

— Daniel Leija

Gay L. Beck

. . . .

Utah Teacher of the Year

. . . .

Kindergarten

. . . .

Highland Elementary School

. . . .

Highland, Utah

Take the time each day to smile and greet each of your students by name, to look into their eyes, and to feel all the possibilities of the day you are starting together.

— Gay L. Beck

Jennifer Lawson

. . . .

Vermont Teacher of the Year

. . . .

7th & 8th Language Arts / Social Studies

. . . .

Vergennes Union High School

. . . .

Vergennes, Vermont

Help students feel supported, challenged, and valued in your class by establishing a connection with each of them. Pay close attention to what they have to say, what they do, and what they work on, so you can engage them through an area of strength or personal interest.

In building this one-on-one relationship, you must be authentic, patient, and willing to listen and to learn from them. This is a time in which you become the student, and they are the teacher. Every student has something magnificent to offer. Discovering what that is just requires that you pay attention.

— Jennifer Lawson

Drema McNeal

. . . .

West Virginia Teacher of the Year

. . . .

6th Language Arts

. . . .

Park Middle School

. . . .

Beckley, West Virginia

Get to know your students as quickly as you possibly can. Learn their names and something about each one of them right from the start of school. Invest your time making each student feel intelligent, important, and loved. Make your classroom a warm and safe environment, a place where your students will want to come. If you can reach them, you can teach them.

— Drema McNeal

Laurie Graves

. . . .

Wyoming Teacher of the Year

. . . .

3rd Grade

. . . .

Big Horn Elementary School

. . . .

Big Horn, Wyoming

Make the effort to understand your students as individuals.   Begin by sending home letters, writing e-mails, and making phone calls before school starts. Invite both parents and students in for a classroom visit or make home calls. Take the time to discover where your students come from — it will give you valuable insight into their world outside of school. Knowing that they are appreciated and cared about as individuals will give your students the confidence to exceed personal and classroom expectations.

Good luck on your journey.

— Laurie Graves

"Education is not the filling of a pail, but the lighting of a fire."

— William Butler Yeats,
Irish poet and playwright

Lead

Darin Curtis

. . . .

California Teacher of the Year

. . . .

8th Physical Education

. . . .

Tierra del Sol Middle School

. . . .

Lakeside, California

Teach your children from the back of the room, as if you were directing a team of dogs pulling a sled. Get out of the way and let the leaders run. The rest of the class will willingly follow them and enthusiastically cover more ground. From the back of the classroom, you will be able to identify who needs the extra assistance to keep up with the pack, while being able to redirect the entire class with a slight pull on the reins.

— Darin Curtis

Diana Fesmire

. . . .

New Mexico Teacher of the Year

. . . .

6th & 8th Mathematics

. . . .

Chaparral Middle School

. . . .

Alamogordo, New Mexico

Empower your students to be advocates for their own learning and members of your learning community. Be a model of a successful learner. Let them see you are not perfect. Allow them to see your mistakes and misconceptions and how you deal with them. My number one expectation for my students and myself: make sense of problems and persevere in solving them.

— Diana Fesmire

Jeff Peneston

. . . .

New York Teacher of the Year

. . . .

Earth Sciences

. . . .

Liverpool High School

. . . .

Liverpool, New York

Teaching is an art form that requires courage, skill, tenacity, experience . . . and a warm human heart. The foundation of the best learning environment is based on respectful teachers building caring relationships with children. Your students will never pass the big exam in June because of any passion you have for the subject. All you can do is lead your students out of the classroom and into nature and ask them to solve problems.

Create settings in which the students teach themselves and discover their own interests, strengths, and passions. If you lead them out into the world, and they find their own passion, strength, and self-confidence there, then the exams will turn out fine.

— Jeff Peneston

*"I expect I shall be a student
to the end of my days."*

— Anton Chekhov,
Russian physician and author

Learn from Others

Timothy M. Dove

. . . .

Ohio Teacher of the Year

. . . .

7th Social Studies / Technology

. . . .

Phoenix Middle School

. . . .

Worthington, Ohio

Seek out the respected teachers in your school and take the time to interview them personally. Ask about their classroom management strategies, their grading procedures, how they connect with students, what they are reading, and how they design lessons and units. Find both individuals teaching what you teach and others who teach other subjects. Use what you learn to design a hybrid approach that will work for you. Be brave and return to these people to discuss ideas and strategies as you work through your first year, always remembering that you are not trying to become the other teacher but rather learning from that teacher to help you find your own voice, your own style as a teacher.

— Timothy M. Dove

*"Nine-tenths of education
is encouragement."*

— Anatole France,
French poet, journalist, and novelist

Look for the Good

Kathy Powers

. . . .

Arkansas Teacher of the Year

. . . .

5th & 6th Language Arts / Reading

. . . .

Raymond and Phyllis Simon Intermediate School

. . . .

Conway, Arkansas

Have amnesia about the past indiscretions of students, and have the memory of an elephant when it comes to acts of kindness, generosity, and brilliance. Avoid being overwhelmed your first year by targeting one area of your curriculum and spending your extra time and resources making it great. The next year, choose a new focus. Master and repeat.

— Kathy Powers

Kristen Lum Brummel

....

Hawaii Teacher of the Year

....

4th Grade

....

Noelani Elementary School

....

Honolulu, Hawaii

Remember that every student who walks into your classroom is someone's child. Treat each and every one of them with the kindness, patience, and compassion that you would lavish on your own child. Reach out to the parents of your students, as they are their first and most important teachers. Know that your partnership with them will guide the children put in your care, allowing them to grow academically, socially, and emotionally into their best selves.

— Kristen Lum Brummel

"The illiterate of the 21st century will not be those who cannot read and write, but those who cannot learn, unlearn, and relearn."

— Alvin Toffler,
American writer and futurist

Pace Yourself

Katy Smith

. . . .

Minnesota Teacher of the Year

. . . .

Parent Education

. . . .

Early Childhood Family Education

. . . .

Winona, Minnesota

Much will be asked of you intellectually, physically, and emotionally this year. Be good to yourself. Think of the school year as a marathon. To be successful, you'll need to pace yourself.

It will be impossible to make it to the finish line without stopping at the watering stations. For teachers, those pit stops are a good night's sleep, food that fuels you, friends that make you laugh, and your own internal coach keeping you focused and fired up.

When you are healthy, it is easy to tap into the passion you have for what you teach. Each year is a new race: be well and enjoy the ride!

— Katy Smith

Shannon Donovan

. . . .

Rhode Island Teacher of the Year

. . . .

9th - 12th Physical Science / Biology

. . . .

Scituate High School

. . . .

North Scituate, Rhode Island

As time wears on, you'll need to have ways to refresh, so you can maintain the enthusiasm you feel for your profession today. Be sure the amount of energy you put into your interactions with students, parents, and all the other people that you deal with daily is sustainable.

Being an educational professional can be emotionally, mentally, and physically challenging, but when it is connected to something you care about deeply, it is much easier to sustain both the energy and interest — for you and for your students.

— Shannon Donovan

LaTonya Waller

. . . .

Virginia Teacher of the Year

. . . .

6th & 8th IB Life / Earth Science

. . . .

Lucille M. Brown Middle School

. . . .

Richmond, Virginia

There is only one first year of teaching — so enjoy it. This is not just a profession; it is also a passion. Pursue it by building relationships with your students that encourage and sustain a positive, successful learning environment. Good classroom management is vital — make it the first thing you teach every year.

The year will be over faster than you think, so take time to journal: "This year is synonymous with drinking water from a garden hose on full blast, but I'm learning how to manage the hose, the water, and spigot better each day!" (From my first year journal.)

— LaTonya Waller

"It is a greater work to educate a child, in the true and larger sense of the word, than to rule a state."

— William Ellery Channing,
Unitarian preacher

Provide the Tools

Kristen Record

. . . .

Connecticut Teacher of the Year

. . . .

9th, 11th, & 12th Physics

. . . .

Frank Scott Bunnell High School

. . . .

Stratford, Connecticut

Have students use pencil on their assignments so it will be easier for them to examine their work — to modify it, expand upon it, correct it, or even erase it and begin again. These are necessary steps in learning. Likewise, remember that as a teacher, what you do in your classroom is not written in permanent ink — never be afraid to ask for an eraser, a do-over. That is when some of the best learning (for you and for them) takes place.

— Kristen Record

"The true teacher defends his pupils against his own personal influence."

— A.B. Alcott,
American teacher and writer

Put Children First

Joseph P. Masiello

. . . .

Delaware Teacher of the Year

. . . .

6th English

. . . .

Cab Calloway School of the Arts

. . . .

Wilmington, Delaware

Upon entering your classroom each morning, leave your ego at the door. Teaching is about the children; always remember that each and every choice or decision you make must be in the best interest of your students. Teaching is all about the kids — not an interrupted planning period or a missed lunch or what makes the teacher comfortable: It's about the children first.

— Joseph P. Masiello

Paul Anderson

. . . .

Montana Teacher of the Year

. . . .

10th - 12th AP Biology

. . . .

Bozeman High School

. . . .

Bozeman, Montana

Demand the undivided attention of all students whenever you are speaking. Never waver in your resolve to improve every day.

And find your students where they are, not where you would like them to be.

— Paul Anderson

Bob Feurer

· ·

Nebraska Teacher of the Year

· ·

7th Science / 11th & 12th Biology, Global Science

· ·

North Bend Central Public School

· ·

North Bend, Nebraska

Stretch. You can't do the same thing every year. You have to keep changing what you're doing in the classroom.

Our jobs are never done as teachers. If you walk into the classroom and you can't see something that could be done better, you probably ought to quit. Strive to be the best you can be every day and hope you pull the kids along with you.

We work for the kids, not for the school board or for the principal or the superintendent. Our employees are our students, and we must believe every day that we're doing the best job we can for them.

— Bob Feurer

"Good teaching is more a giving of right questions, than a giving of right answers."

— Josef Albers,
American educator

Question the Questions

Erika Schmelzer Webb

. . . .

Kentucky Teacher of the Year

. . . .

11th English

. . . .

East Jessamine High School

. . . .

Nicholasville, Kentucky

Rather than giving students the answer when they ask a question, answer their question with a question. Engaging students in a conversation in which they actively reason through the options to the answer they seek is good for their brains. It gets them thinking about what they are asking and why. More importantly, it models the problem-solving process they need to learn so they can solve problems — and find answers — on their own. By you asking them a question, they hear what inquiry sounds like; they participate in it; and eventually they begin to ask the questions themselves before they think to ask you. If they can learn to do this, then they can direct their own learning long after they've left your classroom.

— Erika Schmelzer Webb

"*The teacher who is indeed wise does not bid you to enter the house of wisdom, but rather leads you to the threshold of your mind.*"

— Kahlil Gibran,
Lebanese-American author

Read, Read ... and Read

Dr. Cheryl D. Deaton

. . . .

Tennessee Teacher of the Year

. . . .

4th Grade

. . . .

Pigeon Forge Primary

. . . .

Sevierville, Tennessee

Read, read, read with your students. Create a language-rich, multi-sensory, multi-disciplinary learning space in which students and teacher can learn and grow together.

Find time each day to share a private moment with each student; this will ensure that all students feel safe and secure in your classroom.

Above all remember learning is contagious. As a teacher, remain a passionate, voracious, enthusiastic, and participatory learner! By being personally engaged in learning, you will find it easy to engage your students day after day and year after year.

— Dr. Deaton

*"A teacher should have
an atmosphere of awe,
and walk wonderingly . . ."*

**— Walter Bagehot,
English journalist**

Remember the Wonder

Jay Maebori

. . . .

Washington Teacher of the Year

. . . .

10th - 12th English / Language Arts

. . . .

Kentwood High School

. . . .

Covington, Washington

Keep a rainy day file of cards, notes, letters, and other reminders from former students and parents about the impact you have made on their lives. On those days that we all have, the ones where you question everything — including why you became a teacher or if you're getting through to anyone — pull out your rainy day file and remind yourself that over the years there are people who you have positively influenced. You have made a difference. Now go and create your own rainy day file and begin filling it as soon as you can!

— Jay Maebori

Karen Toavs

. . . .

North Dakota Teacher of the Year

. . . .

8th Language Arts

. . . .

Williston Middle School

. . . .

Williston, North Dakota

The magic of teaching lies in your ability to approach learning with enthusiasm and creativity. Be innovative. Be original. Take time to make sure your classroom is alive with great thinking.

You have chosen a calling in which you can see the wonder; make sure you help your students to see it, too.

Millions of great learning experiences have yet to be designed, so take the creative jump.

— Karen Toavs

"I consider a day's teaching wasted if we do not all have one hearty laugh."

— Anonymous teacher

Set the Mood

Phil R. Wilson

. . . .

Alabama Teacher of the Year

. . . .

1st - 5th Music

. . . .

Ogletree Elementary School

. . . .

Auburn, Alabama

Use music to set the tone for various parts of your students' school day. When they enter the classroom in the morning, have soft, soothing instrumental music playing in the background to help calm them and prepare them for the day's work. Use more energetic music when you see your students are lethargic.

— Phil R. Wilson

Kelly H. Nalley

. . . .

South Carolina Teacher of the Year

. . . .

Elementary Spanish

. . . .

Fork Shoals IB World School

. . . .

Pelzer, South Carolina

Contrary to popular belief, teachers are allowed to smile before Christmas. Smiling offers children encouragement, opens a window into your personality, and provides the first step in creating trust with your students.

Trust builds positive relationships, and positive relationships build the foundation for learning in the classroom. So, smile each and every day, and be sure to demonstrate good character, purpose, and optimism in everything that you do!

— Kelly H. Nalley

"To teach is to learn twice."

— Joseph Joubert,
French moralist

Take Five

Michelle Pearson

. . . .

Colorado Teacher of the Year

. . . .

6th & 7th Geography / 8th American History

. . . .

Hulstrom Options School

. . . .

Northglenn, Colorado

Take five for your profession — and for your students. Take five minutes in the day to turn an "I can't" into an "I can" for a student in your class. Take five minutes to reflect on a practice and to commit to doing it better the next time you teach it. Take five minutes to contact a parent to share the good things his or her child has accomplished at school — rather than the negative.

Take five minutes to reach out to a colleague and complement them on the great things they are doing for their students. Finally, take five minutes to share what is great about being a teacher with a member of the community, someone who may not have children in school but who cares about what is happening in education.

Although these 25 minutes will come out of your

day, they are time well invested, because it is only by working as a team that we will ensure that our students continue to have a bright future ahead of them! And never let anyone tell you something cannot be done, or a child cannot meet a certain level of excellence. It is our job to help every child learn and to reach his or her potential. We can only do this by expecting excellence from each and every one of them, and by modeling professional excellence ourselves. Reach out to your students and learn alongside them.

Help them set goals that will ensure they reach their true potential. Finally, vow to change the words "I can't" to "I can." That is when you have made a lasting impact on a child.

— Michelle Pearson

Teach to Learn

Danielle Kovach

. . . .

New Jersey Teacher of the Year

. . . .

2nd - 4th Special / General Education

. . . .

Tulsa Trail Elementary School

. . . .

Hopatcong, New Jersey

Learn to teach. Teach to learn. These six simple words should embody who you are as a teacher. Your years of education have helped prepare you for teaching. As you enter your classroom, know that your most important lessons will come from your students. They will be your greatest educators. Teach them and learn with them — it's the noblest gift that you could give to your students and to yourself.

— Danielle Kovach

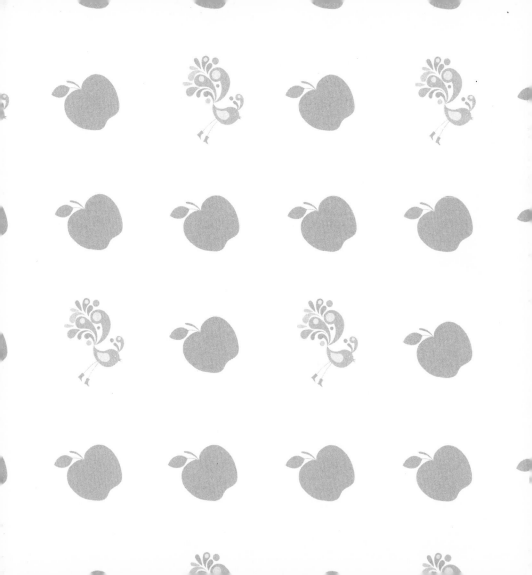